ISBN-13: 978-0692717547
ISBN-10: 0692717544

Published by Andrew Aiton Books

www.andrewaiton.com

GOLDFISH BOAT

By Andrew Aiton

In a lake lived a goldfish who was big as a whale.

As large as he was, he was friendly as a snail.

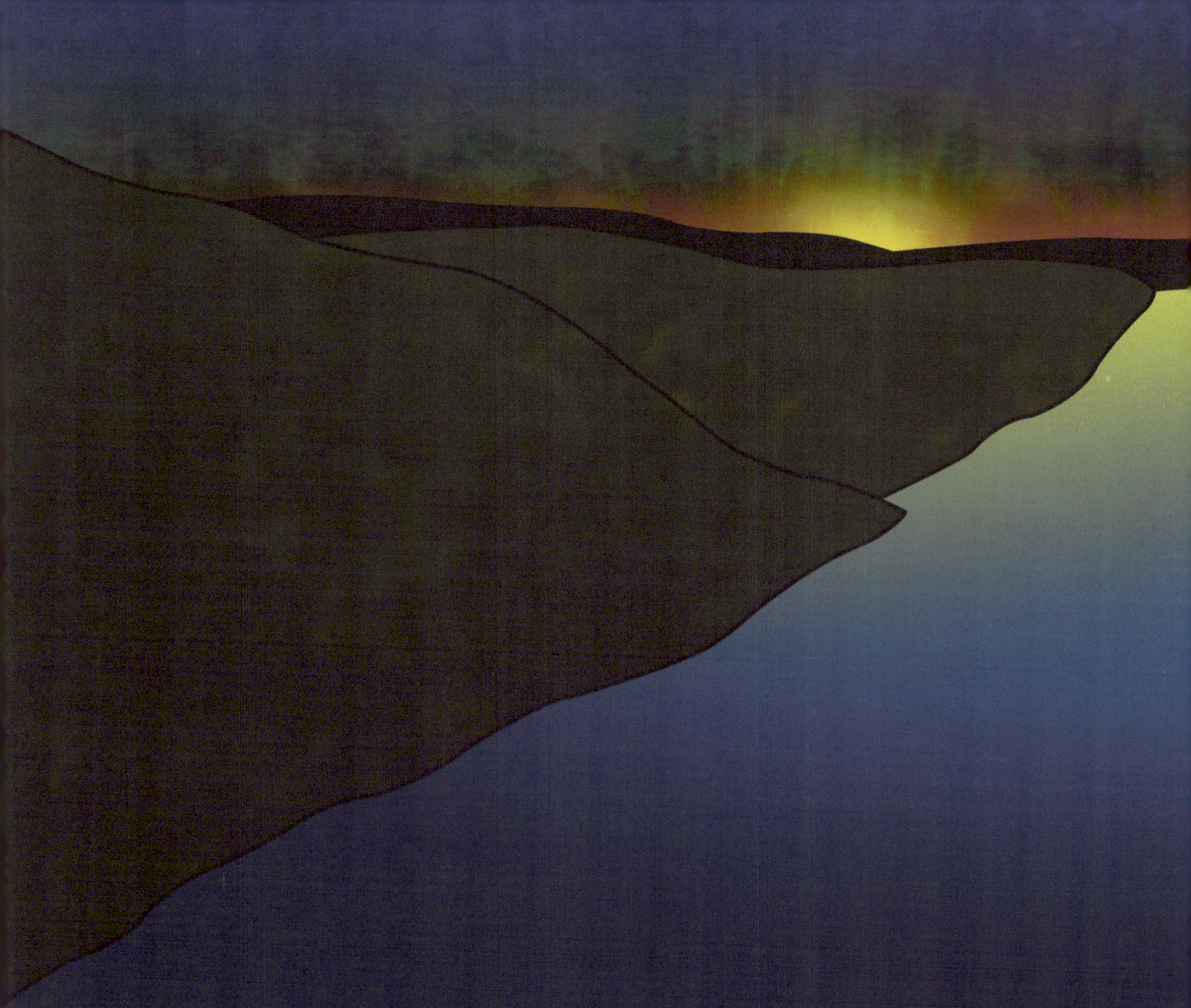

Over the years he had grown ...

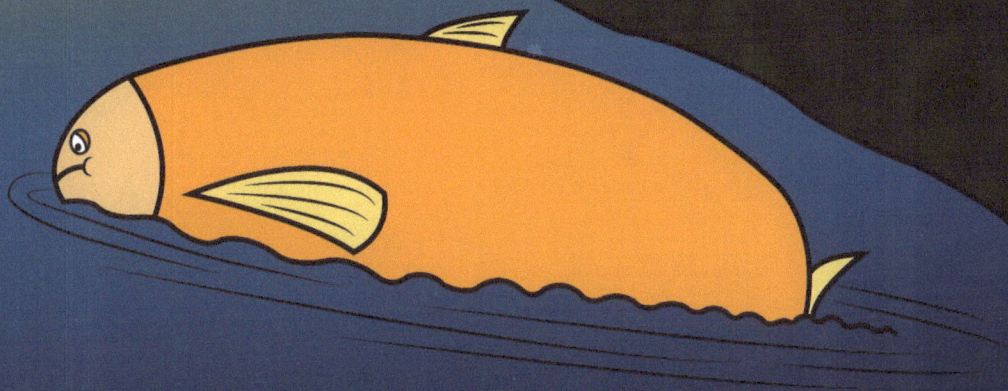

... he was always all alone.

The other animals left the goldfish far from glad.

He had no friends
and was very sad.

One morning a mouse
waved a friendly hello.

This made the
goldfish's day glow.

A powerful storm
blew through.

The animals did not know what to do.

The mouse had an idea that was humble and quick.

The animals climbed onto
the goldfish's back which
was strong and thick.

The animals could stay afloat,

and the goldfish became
a rescue boat!

The animals gave a
warm hug to their
hero and friend.

And the goldfish was happy he now had many friends.

www.ingramcontent.com/pod-product-compliance
Lightning Source LLC
Chambersburg PA
CBHW041243040426

42445CB00004B/134